C000102030

COMPULSIVE

STEVE TAYLOR

To my parents, Danny & Elaine Taylor, my daughter Darcey and my girlfriend Cecelia, with love and gratitude.

Copyright © 2017 Unique Media Group

All rights reserved.

Published by Steve Taylor

www.compulsivebook.com

info@compulsivebook.com

ISBN: 978-1-520568-30-0

CONTENTS

PREFACE

This is my story of how I became a compulsive gambler, and how I escaped from active gambling addiction.

Compulsive gambling, problem gambling or gambling addiction is the urge to gamble continuously even when you know it is doing you harm and you want to stop. According to the NHS, there may be more than 500,000 problem gamblers in the UK.

The thrill of gambling creates a natural high that can become addictive. And with the rise of internet betting, problem gambling is on the increase, particularly among women.

Gambling addiction can lead a person into financial disaster. It can leave the gambler isolated and destroy relationships. Problem gamblers are more likely to suffer from psychological problems such as stress, anxiety, depression and low self-esteem. Gambling can also lead to alcohol abuse. And to fund their activities, gamblers sometimes turn to criminal activity and risk going to prison.

Every day I am grateful for having left gambling behind.

This is a true story, but the names of people I have known have been changed out of respect for their privacy.

1 SURVIVAL

Today life is good. I feel sane and have peace of mind. I am blessed with a beautiful daughter, loving family and a happy and fulfilled life. But this was not always the case. I last gambled over four years ago. That sounds like a long time, but I can remember my last bet just like yesterday.

I first came into gambling recovery more than 12 years ago. I will share with you the events that led me to seek help; I am extremely lucky that I never ended up homeless or behind bars, as my behaviour was getting more and more erratic. At the height of my gambling excess I stole and manipulated people, made a £90,000 bet on a business and even bought shares in a flat-racing horse.

It was complete madness. I was in fantasyland. I was 27 years old, for heaven's sake. What was I playing at? Things were going to come to a head. My life was spiralling out of control. My addiction had me trapped like a hamster in a wheel and I could not stop.

2 THE BEGINNING

Weston-Super-Mare, or Weston-Super-Mud as it's affectionately called in my house, was where we went to on loads of summer day trips out when I was between 7 and 11 years old. My family was never a gambling family, really. My dad did like a bet, but he was never addicted to it, and my mum only really gambles on the lottery. I used to love walking on the old pier, clutching tightly onto my money as I didn't want it to fall through the cracks in the floor and into the sand and sea below.

So, after eating a 99 ice cream, it was time to play on the Derby game which consisted of six horses; if you are in your thirties or forties you will know the game I am talking about. You could put a ten pence stake on and if the outsider won you could scoop three pounds. So I quickly spent all of my money and asked my dad for some more change for the money falls. I loved this game: there was the 2p-a-go version and the 10p version for the big hitters.

I started off on the cheaper game, won a couple of times and decided that I was going to move onto the big boys' silver money falls. It seemed that those 10p pieces must have been glued down, as they were not shifting. Very quickly I had lost all my money. The unfairness of it! I was not having that, so with all the might a seven-year-old could muster I sneakily banged into the machine and about two pounds came out... result! I quickly grabbed my bounty and darted off before the arcade man could see what had happened, but again the money burnt a hole in my pocket and it was gone. This pattern of gambling continued throughout the next four or five years I hated losing on the machines but I knew that I had to play them.

It was like I had no choice. I was drawn to them like a moth to a flame. Looking back, my gambling destiny was being written at seven years old. Even at a young age, if I felt scared or uncomfortable, I would look for distraction. Gambling is such a cunning disease it came in many different guises.

Why did I feel the need to be standing in front of this machine and why did it feel so comfortable?

3 SCHOOL DAZE

I didn't enjoy school very much. I was a quiet child who preferred his own company or the company of a couple of friends. If I had to do anything in front of other students in class I would get very nervous and go into myself. Senior school was more of the same; I was not a confident teenager, I felt awkward and that the girls were not interested in me. Why was this, what was wrong with me?

Thinking back now I think I started to get bullied in the third year of senior school. As I was quiet, and not one of the loud cool kids, they would call me names and sometimes push and shove me. It was the name-calling which hurt me more; I just wished that I could be normal, whatever that is. But I couldn't; I felt like an outsider, and I didn't know how to talk to people. Throughout my teenage years I was quite introverted. I would get embarrassed easily and never fitted in at school.

As time went by I hoped that this awkwardness would go away and that I would start to feel differently, but it didn't, I just felt more isolated. The only time I felt at peace was when I was playing on my computer; I would play obsessively and I hated losing. I started to fight back against some of the bullies and I was left alone and just subjected to name-calling.

I didn't have any girlfriends whilst I was at school. I used to get really shy and nervous around girls, and this just elevated my feelings of not being any good. After final examinations, I decided that I wanted to go to college, and I applied for a First Diploma in Business Studies at Gloucestershire College. For the first time in a long time I felt happy in myself.

It was good to be positive. I was 16 years old and I thought that I was in control of my own destiny. At this moment in my life, everything was good, I felt calm and wanted these thoughts to last. I pretty much breezed through that first year and decided that I would do a National Diploma in Business and Finance, a two-year course. Perfect.

I was slowly finding my feet, but I always seemed to be a person of extremes, either all or nothing, in work, study, friendships and love. I had a good group of friends at this point and a cushy part-time job that was good fun and gave me some beer money. It was at my part-time job that I met Karen, my first proper girlfriend. This would prove to be an exciting but also stressful time in my life, as I didn't have gambling yet to completely distract me.

So college life was pretty good. I felt as if I was learning something which was of value, and I met some really cool and funny people too. We had plenty of time to play pool and unfortunately for me go to the bookies occasionally, but this was all pretty harmless. The bookmakers back then were dark and dingy places. The windows were still blacked out and nearly everyone in there was smoking. It did make me feel that in some strange way I was now more grown up and manly now that I gambled. I worked at a Bingo Hall on couple of evenings in the week and a Saturday afternoon and evening, and that is where Karen worked. Unfortunately, she was engaged to someone else.

The problem was that we got on very well. We had a laugh and she was in charge of me sometimes, which I enjoyed and got a thrill from, but I was in love with her or so I thought. We ended up kissing one New Year's Eve, and then we embarked on an affair for a few months, and then eventually split up. The funny thing was that once I could have her as my girlfriend I didn't really want her; it was all about the chase and the fantasy. She was a lovely girl, but I was

18, thought I was in love and knew it all; it was never going to end well.

Soon I had a decision to make. Did I try and stay on and do a HND course or was it time to go out into the big wide world of work and earn some cash? I decided it was time to get a job, as I had reached my academic limit and didn't fancy another two years or more of studying and being skint. I didn't have a clue what I wanted to do as a career. I managed to get an interview at a Rover dealership in Cheltenham, did OK in the interview with the lady who would be my boss and was offered the job. I now had some sensible money to burn.

4 MY FIRST JOB

I remember starting work, thinking what the hell am I doing here and feeling very much out of my comfort zone. I worked as a warranty administrator with a lovely old chap called Martin who was going to train me up to learn warranty work inside and out. My job was pretty boring. It was doing a number of checks on all the paperwork and checking the mechanics' write-ups, as everything had to be perfect before we put in a warranty claim.

In the office where I worked there were another two men, but mostly women and it was quite a lively environment to work in. Martin had been a service manager in the past but he was now settled as a warranty administrator and only had a couple more years to go before retirement. I also got friendly with Richard, the other lad who worked in accounts, and

Jack who worked in parts. The only problem was that Jack liked to have a bet.

I had only been to the bookies a couple of times before I started my job but that was about to change for good. After my initial worries about whether I would fit, in all was going well but I did get fed with making Martin cups of tea without offering to get me one. Then Jack said about going to the bookies if I wanted; I said that was fine by me.

So the daily routine would consist of Jack and me walking the ten minutes to the bookies, putting on a couple of small bets, and then watching the racing in the canteen in the afternoon whilst Martin would normally fall asleep at the desk. The main thing was to make sure you had a piece of paper in your hand as you walked around: that way you were in the clear. Some things I did learn quickly, especially around gambling.

We carried out with the daily visits to the bookies. It was fairly innocent at this point: literally a couple of pounds a day, and then watching the races we had bet on. The only time I gambled a little bit more is when I was stressed, as I was not very good at dealing with confrontation.

I tended to lose my temper easily or I would sulk if things didn't go my way. I didn't get on very well with the mechanics' foreman. I felt like he would always talk down to me and that whenever I gave him any paperwork to do correctly it took a long time to get it back. I think that we just annoyed each other and that we didn't have any consideration for how each other worked. I found communication generally difficult still at this point; sometimes I wouldn't explain things correctly as I was in a rush with what I wanted to say.

After about nine months from starting the job, Jack mentioned to me that he and a few of his football mates went to the Cheltenham Festival and Gold Cup in March, and that I could go too if I wanted. This all sounded exciting to me. I thought it would be good to have a few drinks and act like a grown up and learn about real gambling. We booked the Tuesday to Friday off work. Back then the Cheltenham Festival was Tuesday to Thursday and we thought we would be somewhat tender on the Friday. Pandora's Box was now almost ready to be opened.

5 THE CHELTENHAM FESTIVAL: A NEW OBSESSION

The Cheltenham Gold Cup and the Festival as a whole is the most prestigious race meeting in England and horse trainers would fly in from France and Ireland to take their chances at the festival. During the Festival, Cheltenham becomes a real party town with the atmosphere buzzing.

My first Cheltenham Gold Cup quickly came around and I did not know what to expect. I had never really experienced race week in Cheltenham before, and the atmosphere in the town that Tuesday morning was electric. It felt like half of Ireland had descended on Cheltenham and the drinks were flowing when breakfast was served. That first day was somewhat of a blur for me, as we slowly made our way from the town centre to the Prestbury Park racecourse via many different bars. I felt different, more grown up; I was in the big leagues now. I hoped I would be lucky.

I remember getting into the Cabbage Patch, as the cheaper enclosure was known then, about an hour before the first race. My adrenaline seemed to have gone up another level with the sheer volume of people and the hustle and bustle. A couple more drinks and then we got into position for the start of the first race. The atmosphere cranked up another level. Then the starter announced 'And they're off!' A massive roar reverberated around Prestbury Park. I suddenly felt that I was now home.

So over the next couple of years I would go to the Gold Cup and a couple of the other meetings, and I would plan my life around Cheltenham race week. My day-to-day gambling had bumped up a little. It was nothing to worry about as yet, but it was certainly becoming a priority in my life. My career had progressed as well. I left Rover after two years, as there were rumours that the company was going to close, and I got my new job as a service administrator at a truck centre in Gloucester. I remember being given this massive folder with all the customers' rates in and thinking 'How the hell am I going to remember all of them?'

I remember feeling terribly anxious when I joined the truck centre. I would go to the toilet at regular intervals and cry that I had made a terrible mistake in leaving Rover. I had always struggled with my emotions. I would blow things up to massive proportions and say to myself that no one liked me at my new job, but these thoughts were not true. The feelings continued for a couple of months, then, after a couple of reprimands from my boss George, I started to find my feet and started working harder. Things started to click into place, and I could remember the different customer rates and systems. We were quite a tight team in the service department, but it was a dog-eat-dog environment, especially with the banter.

At this point, with my shyness, I struggled to communicate with my immediate manager, Sam, and Trevor, the workshop foreman, who was a no-nonsense sort of bloke. But generally we had a good laugh. My old mate Jack ended up joining us at the truck centre, too, when the Rover dealership eventually closed, some nine months after I left.

After three years as service administrator I was doing well and was ambitious, I was offered the position of customer service manager, which brought an increase in pay and a company car. The only problem was that now I had more money, transport, and the ability to go out whenever I wanted, including potentially doing some damage in the bookies. My gambling acceleration didn't happen at once. It crept up on me, and for six to nine months I was in the early stage of addiction.

Feelings of not being good enough lasted throughout my teenage years and on into my early thirties. It was mentally exhausting. My inner voice would be giving out negative self-talk, like 'You have shown yourself up again' or 'You are stupid'. So I would start to seek solace in the bookmakers, because I found out that when I was in the process of gambling you mind would temporarily calm down. Of course, after I had gambled, and lost more money, my mind would be racing even faster: 'How will I pay my rent?', 'How can I pay my bills?' and, most importantly, 'How can I gamble tomorrow?'

6 FACING MY FEARS

I decided to face some of my fears at this point. One
of these was a fear of heights, so when we did a
charity abseil in Gloucester I said I would do it. The
start was the worst thing, when you have to lean back
away from the building but I did enjoy it and there
was plenty of banter with my work mates. I then
decided I was going to do a 20,000 feet tandem sky
dive for Winston's Wish, which is a charity for
bereaved children. The skydive was at an aerodrome
in Northampton and I went along feeling very
nervous but trying to put on a front that I was OK. I
remember having to wait a few hours as it was quite
windy, but eventually we were told that we would be
going up in an hour's time. The small aeroplane we
were in was like something out of Indiana Jones and
there were six of us in the plane, two of us doing

tandem sky dives with our instructors and two people doing static jumps at 10,000 feet.

As the plane started along the runway, it was all very much dream-like and I was feeling quite calm; that is, until we approached 10,000 feet. A young lad was somewhat excitable. As he was getting ready to jump out he was banging the side of the plane and then he jumped, quickly followed by the other static parachute jumper. It was at this point that reality dawned on me. I was heading towards 20,000 feet in this tiny aeroplane and I was going to dive out. I had only wanted to brag to my mates that I had done a skydive; now the reality of the situation was kicking in. What had I been thinking?

We ascended to 17,000 foot, 18,000 foot, 19,000 foot. The instructors started to move us near the door. Bloody hell we're doing this! I thought it would be cool to do a skydive, what the hell? My instructor asked me if I was OK. I felt like telling him to bugger off but I gave him the thumbs up and we were out first. I remember putting my feet outside the plane and throwing myself forward. We were falling like a meteor from out of space. I was buzzing at this point. We must have been freefalling for around a minute; then we opened the chute. What a glorious view of Northampton! I could see for miles, and the instructor gave me the guide ropes so I could change our direction. Before long we had landed and I was exhilarated and stayed that way for the rest of the week. I was somewhat of an adrenaline junkie during this period of my life. I was looking for validation, concerned with what others thought about me, because I thought so little of myself at this time.

With the customer service manager role, I really enjoyed it as it meant visiting existing clients and also winning new clients, which gave me a thrill when I managed to sign someone up. The first six months of the role were going well, as I wanted to impress George, and I was focused on the job in hand. I would pop into the bookies on occasion but nothing too drastic; but it was only a matter of time. I remember visiting one particular existing client and he really gave me a hammering as we had let them down. I felt really embarrassed, and didn't know what to say, and I ended up spending quite a lot in the bookies that day.

I then got into a daily routine where I would do some admin in the office first thing, then go out and visit clients and prospects for a few hours. Then I would spend around two hours or so in the bookies, not every day to start with but it slowly became that way. At this moment in time I could afford to lose what I was gambling. I was living at home still and had disposable income, but some days I would over step the mark and create a temporary problem. I did quite well as a customer service manager and after a year I was asked if I could help out at our Worcester location as the lady manager there was struggling. It was becoming quite a big concern.

I was quite excited. I knew that this would be a good opportunity to impress George, and I didn't want to let him down. So I knuckled down over the next month or six weeks and really got to grips with the garage; I felt that I had made a difference.

One day I was called on the phone by the managing director, Edward, who said that he wanted to meet me at a pub about 10 miles away from the branch and that I was not to tell anyone that I was meeting him.

My mind was racing. Had somebody seen me going into the bookies when I should have been working? Or did someone see me at Cheltenham races when I had phoned in sick? Why didn't he want to meet me at the garage?

I got there and Edward and my manager George were in there waiting for him. I thought I was really in for a kicking.

'All right, Steve, how's things?' said Edward. 'Do you want something to eat? George and I are having something.'

I was thinking 'Yes please,' but Edward was somewhat erratic so I thought I might still get into trouble, and was still on edge.

'So how do you like working in Worcester so far?'

'I like it. I enjoy dealing with the customers and working with the staff.'

'What about Ann. How is she getting on?'

I started to relax a bit now as it looked as if I was in the clear. 'She seems to work hard,' I said. 'But it is not easy, as some of the workshop lads give her the run around and she is busy costing up jobs.'

'Well, we are not happy with how things are going, Steve. We have big plans for Worcester and it looks like we will be asking Ann to step down.'

At this point I asked myself whether they were thinking of offering me the job. I had just turned 25, it would have been my first managerial job, and Worcester was growing every week. George said to me that they thought I could do the job, that they would offer it to me on an interim basis and if I did well I would get it full time. Wow! To say I was stunned was an under-statement. But I was excited, and thought that with some training and development I could do well, as I was enthusiastic and wanted to prove myself. So over the next three months I knuckled down and did really well. I put systems back in place, got most of the technicians onside and was offered the job on a permanent basis. During this period I hardly gambled, as I was focused on doing a good job and showing my boss that I was capable.

Unfortunately the extra money I received as a service manager was extra ammunition in the bookies, as I struggled at times with three of the technicians who were on a downer with the company and not really prepared to give me a chance. They would be sarcastic and sometimes I handled it OK and other times I didn't. I used gambling as a release from the stress of the job. The problem was that my gambling increased and my time out of work went up too, which meant more stress, because when I went into work I had to play catch up. My ego was starting to get out of hand and it was at this point that I thought about buying a racehorse.

7 DYNAMIC B

By now I had started going to other racecourses, in addition to 95 per cent of the meetings at Cheltenham; I went to Stratford, Exeter, and one year to the Derby at Epsom. All fairly innocent fun, really, apart from that I got delusions of grandeur and thought I was somewhat of a horse expert. I started seriously considering buying shares in a horse. I started checking the *Racing Post* and researching information on buying horses. I learned that there was a three-year-old flat horse that had become available to buy and that a London-based syndicate was looking for another member.

I called up the chap who was organising the syndicate and arranged to meet him and Ian the horse trainer at their training HQ in Lambourn. We watched the horse on the gallops. It was all very exciting, and I quickly became seduced into the idea of getting shares in this horse and it winning some races. I said I was in, and I now had one-eighth share in a racehorse called Dynamic B. It cost me £2,000. I was earning around twenty-five grand a year at this point. What the hell was I playing at? But by now my grasp on what was normal and what was fantasy was more blurred by the day. At this point I was quite conscientious at work, but not for much longer, as work would start to get in the way of my gambling.

I tried to get down to see the horse train at least twice a month and I would take my Dad down as he was into his horses too. We used to really enjoy ourselves, but I got caught by the police once near Swindon doing over 100 miles per hour as we were running late to see the horse cantering. I had to go to court and thankfully I only got a temporary driving ban of about six weeks. I also had the shame of the local paper printing my words to the policeman: '106 miles per hour, I didn't think I was going that fast.' The shame of it!

After two or three months went by I realised that I couldn't afford to continue my share in the horse, as there were additional costs when she was entered into a race. So I spoke to Ben the syndicate leader and he thankfully bought my share in the horse so I could concentrate on my daily gambling addiction in the bookies. I was now slowly spiralling out of control as

I had also started betting on the roulette machines in the bookies and you could lose a lot of money very quickly.

8 ROULETTE

Roulette is known as the crack cocaine of gambling due to how quickly you burn money and how it can accelerate your addiction, which was certainly true in my case. It started innocently enough. I had seen the machines in the bookies for a good six months and never really paid too much attention to them before. I think I was waiting for a horserace one day and thought to myself 'Let's have a quick go on the roulette'. I got the bug almost straight away, I think it was because you know almost instantly if you have won or lost. I thought that I had worked out a system of when certain numbers came up, but as usual it was just an excuse just to keep gambling.

Very quickly I had started gambling more on the roulette machine than I did on the horse racing. I also kidded myself that it paid out on certain numbers in a sequence and I started to write down all the winning numbers. It was bloody madness. I would then follow this so-say routine and win a couple of times then end up losing a small fortune. The good thing was that by using the roulette machines that it brought me to Gambling Recovery quicker and helped me to get the help needed.

So a normal day in Worcester was spending an hour with my team, making sure everything was happening as it should be, and then me vanishing for a real or imaginary sales appointment. Then it was into the bookies for three or four hours minimum to gamble on the horses or on the roulette. That was really my drug of choice now, as you didn't have to wait for the horses to run, you just picked your numbers and spun the wheel and win or lose. This would go on till mid-afternoon when I would head back to work.

I remember there was a guy in my regular bookies who could tell you what number the ball was going to land on as soon the roulette wheel started to spin. I wished he would clear off, but he was just waiting for me to leave the machine so he could win some of the money I had just blown.

Another thing that stands out clearly from this time is that my monthly bank statements would be about 20 pages long, owing to the number of withdrawals I would make every day. I would take out

£50, quickly lose it, then take another walk down Worcester High Street to take out another £40. If I won, I would go back and pay back £50 into the bank. I would think I was even and just playing with the money I had just withdrawn. The £40 would be quickly lost and I would be back at the cash machine again. This was a daily ritual for me; I would get angry and shout, but I couldn't stop gambling.

9 IN A BAD PLACE

This daily routine went on for about two years. I don't really know how I was not caught, as I got more blatant as time went on. Because I was never in work I would have loads of issues and problems to sort, so I got stressed and needed to gamble, and on and on it went. I was in quite a depressed state at this point. I had stolen some small amount of money from work, but I was stealing hours from them every day when I had been gambling. It was at this point that I decided I was going to be a professional gambler and I had worked out what I was going to bet on. So I visited the bank and told them that I needed a loan to buy a new car and some debt consolidation. I was lying. I just wanted the money. I managed to get a loan for £18,000 and I was waiting for it to hit my bank account.

I was having a particularly bad day at work, dealing
with a few difficult technicians, when I checked my
bank account and found out that the £18,000 had
cleared. My head was swimming. I was fed up with
feeling stressed all the time at work. Of course, I was
stressed because I was spending 30 hours a week in
the bookies, so I was having to do my 50-hour job in
20 hours. When I should have been working and
managing the staff, I was gambling. Gambling will
have an impact on your job, maybe not straight away.
It affected my mental health, the constant juggling of
work, gambling, life. I was struggling badly and the
cracks were starting to show.

At dinner time, I put my phone, works mobile and
car keys on my desk and walked out. I slowly made
my way to Worcester Shrub Hill train station by foot,
thinking what I was going to say to Tracey, my
girlfriend at the time. But I would worry about that
later. I had a load of cash: what was I going to gamble
on first?

My own mobile phone was going mad at this
point. My boss, George, was ringing me up every 15
minutes and it was making me feel uncomfortable, as
the call was bringing me back into the real world. I
had walked out of a good job that I had been at for
eight years. What had I done? I called my Dad and
was talking to him about it, but I must admit
everything was a bit of a blur. I decided to speak to

George, and agreed to meet up with him in a couple of days' time. I went home and spoke to Tracey about what happened, but I was in a haze, so I'm not sure what I exactly said to her. But I decided that I was going to repay the £18,000 loan, as surely that was the sensible thing to do.

I met my boss at Tesco's café on Tewkesbury Road, Cheltenham. George could see I was in a bad place. I told him half of the truth that I was having a tough time with family problems and the stress of the job had sent me over the edge. George was really understanding and I felt that I maybe able to turn the work situation round. We agreed that I would go back into Worcester on Monday and see how I get on. I felt really embarrassed when I went back in, as I was the depot manager and I had walked out. One technician made a smart remark but apart from that I was welcomed back to work. I realised now that I had to do something about my gambling, as I knew it had been my main problem. I started investigating what help was available. George decided that I would be better off working at the Hereford garage, as it was much smaller and easier to manage, but it was also good that I had customer service experience as we wanted to increase the number of clients.

I remember calling a gambling helpline to try and find out what was available to me as I was keen to stop gambling and get control of my life. I was told that there was a gambling recovery meeting in Gloucester every Monday evening and I said I would go along. I told Tracey that I had a gambling problem and I didn't really know how to stop, but that I had been told about gambling meeting and that I would go along soon. It took me about two months to work up the courage to go to a Gamblers Recovery meeting. If I am honest I thought the room was going to be full of down-and-outs and bums.

My life was slowly unravelling at this point. I was worried that I was going to end up stealing a large amount of money, or that I would end up homeless or even in prison, as my behaviour was out of control when I was gambling. Something had to change.

10 GAMBLING RECOVERY

So there I was in the Gloucester Gamblers Recovery meeting. I had been putting it off for a few months, but it was time to front up and see what it was all about. I couldn't carry on as I was. It was quite a hard place to find, and I was just about to call it quits when I eventually came across the venue. It is used as a drop-in centre during the day.

There were a couple of people outside and a young lad got talking to me and asked me what my vice was. I said it started off on the horses but the roulette had killed me. He was a really nice guy. He said he dealt with antiques and had been coming to the meeting for about six months. It put me a little bit at ease and I walked into the room for the first time. There were about 10 people there and I was shocked to see that most of them looked like normal people and not the down-and-outs that I had imagined would be there. I relaxed a little.

The meeting got started, and one of the older, more experienced members, who was chairing, went round the room to take people's names and when they last gambled. I mumbled my name, and when everyone had introduced themselves Mr A spoke to me. He asked me to answer the 20 questions used by the organisation to see if I had a problem with compulsive gambling. I think I scored about 15 or 16; most compulsive gamblers score a minimum of seven. I was in the right place all right.

The chairman asked me to talk about my current situation to explain what had brought me to Gambling Recovery. I was really nervous, but managed to talk about the fact that however hard I tried I just couldn't stop gambling and that I owed about £5,000 at this point. There were some big characters in the room and there was also some banter flying round. But everybody was pretty friendly and gave me loads of tips about how to stop gambling.

They also said I should find someone I trusted to take charge of my money. My initial thoughts were 'sod that'. I wasn't going to give Tracey my bank cards. She didn't have a clue how much I was earning and she certainly had no idea I was gambling hundreds of pounds every month. I was hoping that a few of these characters could tell me how I was gambling wrong so I could have a better go at doing it correctly. That's the warped mind of a compulsive gambler!

At this point I still wanted to gamble on a social level. I just needed to learn how to stop gambling every day. So to be told that I couldn't gamble on anything ever again was a shock to the system to begin with. But I did want to get my life back on track, so I was prepared to give it a go and week by week I got into the programme and started speaking a little more. After a couple of months, I started getting friendlier with a few of the members and after we had washed up the cups we would go for a pint and talk in more detail in a slightly relaxed environment. Things were going pretty well for me, but unfortunately the Cheltenham Gold Cup was round the corner and I wasn't ready to walk away from it just yet.

So there I am in the Gambling Recovery meeting, the evening before the Tuesday start of the Gold Cup, as happy as Larry, because I knew I would be going gambling at Cheltenham the next day. I had also created a split with Tracey on the Monday. My desire to gamble was more than my desire to be with her, so I had moved all my barriers out of the way. All that was left was to tell Jack I would be going to the races. He seemed a bit confused as I had told him previously about my problem but I soon talked him round. I told him that the boys were back and we would have a good time. When gambling gets hold of me it is like a force of nature, almost unstoppable. You will do unthinkable things so you can have your fix. Nothing matters except gambling.

We arranged to meet up for breakfast and a drink in town, get our bets sorted in town, and then to have a few more drinks before heading up to the racecourse. We decided in the end that we would stay in town and watch the races instead and would go up on Wednesday and Thursday. I ended up winning a race and left Jack in the pub while I went to get my money. I was doing OK up to this point, gambling normally and managing to keep a lid on things. But I decided I wanted to have a quick go on the roulette machine …

In a blink of an eye I had done a load of cash and I felt like shit. Reality was dawning that I could not stop once I got started. I remember getting the bus home and getting off near the Cross Hands Pub in Cheltenham and contemplating just walking out in front of a car to just end it all. I felt terribly low and depressed but I still went to the racing for the rest of the week and would hide away from Jack on the roulette machines or gamble more on horses when he wasn't nearby.

On the Friday evening I went round to Tracey's and explained what had happened. I said I was sorry and that I would go back to Gambling Recovery again on the Monday. I thought I was at rock bottom and that I never wanted to gamble again. And that's what I did. For seven-and-a-half years exactly I was abstinent. No gambling, but my life was still unmanageable. I told the group that I had had my last bet on the Friday 18 March 2005. I got somewhat of a grilling, but I did want to stop this time.

11 STOPPING GAMBLING:
THE FIRST TIME

So I went back to Gambling Recovery and told them
that I had been gambling at Cheltenham Races but I
really wanted to stop. So I started to pay more
attention in the meetings as I now realised the
seriousness of my illness. I knew that gambling would
chew me up and spit me out if I relapsed again. Work
had sorted itself out in Hereford and over the next 12
months I had really settled down. Then, in March
2006, Tracey called me at work to say she was 99 per
cent sure she was pregnant. We had both managed to
save some money and we bought our house ready for
when our child was born.

   I was really starting to take on some responsibility
and I was managing well with not gambling or
wanting to gamble. But the danger was that I was

cherry picking from the Recovery programme, only working on those that I wanted to and not in the order that they should be done. Then, on 26 December 2006, my beautiful daughter was born and I was so protective of her it gave me extra motivation to stay clean and to better myself. My only real issue was that my relationship with my fiancée was slowly breaking down. We were both enjoying being parents but we had been growing apart for some time.

I was really finding my voice now in Recovery meetings and I would even occasionally take on the chairman's role, which was good as it made me listen better to what everyone was saying. I was also starting to look for a job nearer to home as I wanted to see as much as possible of my daughter. Two years' abstinence from gambling went by without any real dramas but something wasn't right. I was still a person of extremes. Whether it was flirting with women on a night out with friends, or drinking too much, or going on a dating site, what was I doing? I spoke to my fiancée about not being happy and we both had a good cry and promised that we would work harder at our relationship. I didn't want to leave my daughter as I adored her.

I ended up leaving the truck centre in Hereford and started work at a fast fit garage in Cheltenham. The money was brilliant, but it quickly became apparent that they wanted us to lie to our customers to get them to have tyres, brakes, and exhausts replaced when in reality these weren't necessary. I hated working there. I was not willing to put my name to something dishonest. I called George, my old boss, and said that I had made a mistake and told him all about the new job. I asked him if there were any other jobs going in Worcester or Gloucester and thankfully they were creating a new position and I was fast tracked into the vacancy.

I was so happy that I could escape the fast fit job and go back to the truck centre. My job was administration manager for both Hereford and Worcester. The good thing was that I only had to go over to Hereford twice a week and it was less stressful than my old job. Generally having less stress was good for me; when I was under pressure I felt like I was more likely to gamble, and I didn't like having those feelings. Things were still not great at home. We both loved being parents, but us as a couple we had gone backwards. Also I was starting to change as a person and was not the bloke that she had met five years ago. I felt alive to what was going on in the world. Whereas before I felt as if I could only see the world in black and white, now I could see it in colour and surround sound.

The next couple of years were pretty good. I was feeling like I no longer wanted to gamble anymore and I was starting to feel calmer in myself, even thou

I could get excitable in Gambling Recovery meetings and give a few people a tongue lashing. I was now chairing meetings on a regular basis and starting to feel like I was progressing in my recovery, but I was still very much capable of extreme behaviour. I could be very much all or nothing. The one thing which was starting to drip into my mind was that I wanted to start my own business. I decided that I would start my own car garage within the next 12 months. My fiancée was not impressed with this at all, but my mind was made up. I wanted to create something for me and my family.

Looking back now it was another nail in our coffin as we were heading in opposite directions. I had found my ambition and wanted to better myself and my family. I was now aware that I would have to split up with my fiancée, as we were no longer in love, but the thought of not seeing my daughter every day was heartbreaking. I was very much devoted to my daughter, but I did want to be happy, as life is so precious and flies by so quickly. I spoke about my personal situation to other people in Gambling Recovery as I wanted to get another perspective before I made such a big decision. I knew that I was going to leave the family home but I wanted to be reassured.

It was Spring 2010 when I sat with my fiancée and said that I was going to leave, as I was not happy; she admitted that she was not happy either. We agreed that I would be able to see my daughter every week and that I would be able to call her most days too. I wanted to leave the house for my ex to raise our daughter in, and I was confident that I would make a success out of my car garage and that I would be OK.

So I found a two-bedroom flat to rent and I moved out. I can remember the last time I was in the house. I was very emotional and I just hugged my daughter tightly. Then, when she was fast asleep, I left the house and I cried all the way round to my mum's house as I was staying there for a few days until the flat was ready. Leaving my daughter was the hardest thing I have ever done. It broke my heart, as I knew I would not be able to see my beautiful daughter every day, but I couldn't stay in the relationship.

12 TAYLOR COMMERCIAL SOLUTIONS

I had worked my one month's notice at work and was in the process of finding the right location for the garage and also the funding to make sure that I could make the garage a long-term reality. I had a look at several locations and got gazumped by another well known company. I then came across the units at Neptune Business Centre in Cheltenham.

First of all I was shown a smaller unit of about 2,000 square feet. It didn't have a separate office but I did like it. But as soon as I walked into Unit 5 I knew this is where I wanted to be. It was 4,000 square feet and had a downstairs office.

When Simon the agent took me upstairs, and I looked out the window across the estate, I felt like I was Scarface and that this was my kingdom to conquer. Not that I had a God complex or anything.

Us compulsive gamblers are complicated buggers.

I knew that as long as I got a personal loan, a business loan, and some investment I would be able to afford it. Looking back now it was sheer lunacy; addict behaviour with no grip on reality. I was a start-up business with no customers. What on earth was I doing in a 4,000 square feet unit?

Abstinence and recovery are two completely different animals. Abstinence is just not gambling. Recovery is working on your character defects so you are less likely to gamble again or seek out destructive behaviour elsewhere. Recover is the difficult part: it takes real effort to change your habits. I may have been more than five years gambling free, but my decision-making was pure fantasy. The whole business idea belonged in a bad novel, but it had become very real and once I got a taste of the big time I was obsessed.

I had started off the lending process with NatWest, trying to get business loan. But after a couple of initial meetings I didn't really get anywhere with them. They were not interested. So I went into Lloyds and met one of their corporate business managers. The chap was a nice guy and I think my enthusiasm encouraged his interest. They were quite receptive to what I was looking to achieve. I had to make several amendments to my business plan and get five letters of intent from prospective clients, which I managed to achieve. The garage and the building were now something of an obsession. I was going to make my mark on the world so if Lloyds' manager wanted me to rewrite the business plan 20 times that is what I would do.

I also went to a local organisation called Fredericks Foundation, which helps people who can't get funding through the banks. I got through the first initial phases and made it to the lenders' meeting. Now this was interesting. It was a real Dragons Den scenario with myself and 12 people on the panel. They questioned my business plan and fired a few hardcore questions, but I think I handled myself quite well. I didn't make it through to getting a loan, though, as I said that I was still speaking to Lloyds and it looked promising.

Not long after the panel I had secured a personal loan of £12,000 and two friends would invest about £40,000 between them if I could get the business loan for another £40,000, which as far as I was concerned was going to happen. I had decided that it would go through and it felt like the Bank Manager was pitching for me as well. The whole process took around six weeks from the beginning to the business loan being signed off; the loan was confirmed by Lloyds and was underwritten by the European Trust. I was now in business as far as I was concerned. I was as high as a kite afterwards. I felt so proud of myself.

Getting the money from Lloyds was like mission impossible at times but I had not let myself quit.

I got in touch with the agent and emailed over my offer for reduced rent and lease breaks on the 4,000 square feet unit. I think they must have thought it was their lucky day as I signed up for a seven-year lease in a recession. My initial thought was that I wanted a mechanic as a business partner; they would run the workshop and I would build the customer base as I could not repair any vehicles myself. I was prepared to learn some basics to help out, but the technicians backed out when it came to signing their names.

I sometimes wonder what would have happened if I'd asked them why they didn't go for it, if they had said it was over-ambitious and too risky. Would I have listened to them and pulled out? Probably not. I decided in my own great wisdom that I would take the unit on and create an amazing garage and it was me against the world again, not the best idea in retrospect. In hindsight the garage was the biggest gamble I had ever placed, as I was betting £92,000 on my ability to build something for the long term. But looking at my business plan, I was way over-optimistic with my proposed sales. And unfortunately I had misjudged some of the main costs, including rates and the cost of advertising and promoting the business.

When the doors opened I started the business with

a young technician and an experienced technician and slowly we started to get work from the estate we were on and different friends and family members, but the business was haemorrhaging money because the costs were much higher than the sales. I would log onto the business bank account every morning and it would be quite stressful seeing the balance dropping. The problem was that a series of fundamental errors had set me up to fail: the size of the premises, the cost of lease hire equipment, an electrical refit of more than £12,000 and a bill of more than £3,000 for builders' work. My mind was not in reality at this point, it was in fantasy. I was hoping that I would be able to get sales over £20,000 every month – and that was never going to happen. I managed to win a couple of good business accounts after six months that helped to build sales figure but I was still losing around £4,000 every month. I was nose-diving my way to the ground.

Unfortunately, I was completely disconnected with that reality. I was walking round like I had made it: Steve Big Bollocks who owns his garage. I was somebody now. I was really arrogant in Gambling Recovery meetings; I would be loud and obnoxious. I was happy to give someone a verbal beating, to tell them where they had gone wrong. I always knew best, didn't I? In reality, I needed a loving arm round the shoulder and some words of guidance instead of my ego. I thought I am Steve, I am 35 years old, I own my own business, I have a fantastic girlfriend, I am an amazing bloke: it was complete egotistical bullshit. I was setting myself up for a massive fall, which I didn't see coming. More likely, I refused to see it coming.

But there were some great times too. I started speaking to a lady called Katherine on an internet dating site in late December 2010 and we decided that I would meet her in Harrow on 3 January. I was really excited, as we got on well when we talked on the phone and we had some really good chemistry. We met up and we got on great from day one. We had loads of things in common, we shared very similar values, and we made each other laugh. I thought she was stunning.

At the beginning, we would meet up every weekend when I didn't have my daughter, and that soon progressed to meeting up in the week. I was completely in love at this point, but I could not tell her that the business was struggling. I had to keep up the pretence that all would be well with it.

The funny thing is that I really enjoyed the garage but I was also completely obsessed with it, morning, noon and night. Which for a compulsive gambler is not a great thing. It is important to have your life balanced: work, family, friends, relationships, hobbies and most importantly my recovery, because without recovery everything is screwed. But I was obsessed

with the business and spending time and money on
my daughter and Katherine.

13 NO LONGER SOLVENT

I managed to get some additional investment from one of my friends, as the sales had actually dropped off somewhat and I was now paying full rent. That morning bank balance check was extremely painful. But me and the girlfriend were getting on great. I was hoping that I could convince her to leave London and come and live with me in Cheltenham as she was the person that I wanted to be with.

Then one day in early June I got a telephone call from my accountants; they wanted me to go over to their offices in Gloucester. My mind was swimming. I spoke to the lads and said I had to pop out for a bit and I headed over to Gloucester. I got to the offices, and my accountant, a nice lady called Jane, said that she wanted me to speak to Jim, the owner. Jim wasn't into small talk. He just hit me with it: 'Steve, I have been going through your last statements and cashflow. You are going to have to stop trading. You are no longer solvent.'

'Jim,' I said, 'I can turn this round. I only need a couple of good months and I will be fine.' What the hell was I on about? Jim basically spelled it out that unless we could turn over £25,000 we would have to wind up the company. The size of the task hit me and I said there was no way we could do those figures. Jim could see I was shell-shocked. He got Jane to make me a drink and started discussing what I would have to do to wind up the business. He knew a firm of liquidators in Cheltenham and gave me their details. I would have to ring them within the next couple of days and get things in place for winding up the business.

I felt sick to my stomach, as I knew I had no way out of this situation. I would have to go back and tell my staff that I was going to have to close the garage and that they would need to find new jobs. This was my real rock bottom moment. Looking back on it now, I felt as if I was in a car crash; everything felt like it was in slow motion. I went back and told my mechanics and explained that they would be paid for the work they had done, but they would need to get new jobs. I knew that with all the personal guarantees I gave on the rent, business loans and equipment finance I would have to go bankrupt. I was horrified.

I called this liquidation company and had a meeting with one of the managers. He was really blasé about everything, asking me if I wanted to do a phoenix and start again. I knew I was in a hole for over £80,000 in loans, equipment and rent. I was screwed. I just told him that there was no way that I was going to start again; the whole episode was a nightmare. I had to go back to the garage a couple of times as the equipment companies were collecting the ramps; I had to watch them dismantled and taken away. This was too much for me to deal with. I was heartbroken. Meanwhile, Katherine was moving to Cheltenham to live with me.

I started looking for work and eventually started found a job at a truck rental company as workshop administrator. It was OK but my head was still in a state of shock. I was in mourning at the death of my business, but I was happy that I was with my girlfriend and she had managed to get a job almost straight away.

I sucked it up at the truck rental company for about six months and then I left and tried to start my own garage again in smaller premises, operating out of a small agricultural shed in Shurdington and then a garage off the lower High Street in Cheltenham. We had moved to Albert Street in St Paul's, which again in hindsight was a bad decision, as the house was old, damp and neither of us liked the area.

14 IN BUSINESS AGAIN

So after being made bankrupt and burning up the best part of £90,000 in a year, I wanted to start a garage again. What a bloody fool! The only reason I did it was down to my own stupid pride after failing the first time round. I wasn't a mechanic, so I would always have to pay someone to do the work. It was crazy. I managed to keep the unit for around five months, but by then the work had not picked up enough. I realised then that I shouldn't have started the garage again. Thankfully my landlord was a sensible man and after giving me a reprimand he let me leave the unit. I felt bad, as part of my desire to start another business was to pay back money that a friend had invested in the first business.

This period was a real tough time, as my decision-making was terrible, and I compromised my relationship with my girlfriend Katherine to try and keep the business going. I remember that I took my last £10 to go to a networking event in the evening, when the electricity was just about to run out. (Due to a falling out with the utility provider, we had to have a prepayment electricity meter to service the debt and current use. It cost us a fortune when we were struggling financially.)

I was only concerned with the possibility of earning some money through the networking event and completely overlooked the fact that there would be nothing left on the meter so Katherine would be OK to cook her meal. But when I got back the house was in darkness and she was going mad as she had had to eat her food in the dark. So I raced round to the corner shop and got some credit put on the card.

Due to this period of being self employed and leaving jobs I had put a lot of pressure on my girlfriend, even to the case that even going out for a meal was a massive luxury. The pressure had started coming in my mind as I was desperate for money but didn't want to work for anyone. It was at this point that I ended up relapsing in my recovery, on 15 November 2012.

15 RELAPSE

I had done it again, after everything I had been through and the trust I had rebuilt. Seven-and-a-half years of abstinence down the drain and for what? Eight pounds in the roulette machine. How had it come to this after all that time away from gambling?

If I am honest I could see the bet coming though. As sure as night follows day, it had been building up to that point for months. Sometimes you don't see the devil when he comes looking for you, as he comes disguised as drink, workaholic, sexual attraction or whatever is your drug of choice.

Mine was always distraction: anything to stop me thinking about the decisions I was making. And believe me, decision-making was never my strong point. But why did my mind want me distracted? What was I running away from? Back to 15th

November 2012 and the lead-up to my relapse.

Two months previously when I was working at the truck rental garage and the lure of gambling came calling again. I made up some bullshit excuse about my father being ill, just so I could get my fix. I couldn't get to the bookies quickly enough; it was like I was possessed. I was in autopilot; it was like I floated in through the doors. I couldn't get the £20 into the machine quick enough, but then I was thinking 'Christ, you haven't gambled for almost eight years. What are you doing?' So I pressed the refund button and took my money out, but the damage was done. That day had been coming for a while, as relapses are not flukes; my life had still been unmanageable while I had been abstinent from gambling.

So that takes us to 15th November 2012, the last time I gambled. I had been manipulating Katherine for a few weeks, suggesting that for me to gamble again would help us out with our chronic lack of money, which was due to me starting a business I should never have started, as I had no cashflow and no other income at all. But on the day in question I kidded myself that I would only gamble a maximum of £5 on the roulette machine and then I would walk away while up. The problem was that I had £20 on me. And £5 doesn't last long when you are a compulsive gambler. I then took our last £15 out of my wallet and blew that away too. I felt terrible. What the hell was going on with me? I felt physically sick. Seven-and-a-half years of abstinence gone just like that. What the fuck was I doing? Why did I keep hurting myself and those close to me? My poor girlfriend, the lady that I loved, was being manipulated, conned and cheated. Who was I starting to become?

But as you will find out, this behaviour was my normal. I had been a crazy dude for as long as I could remember. But being crazy is cool, isn't it? I always wanted to be cool from as far back as I can remember. But this wasn't cool for anybody, not for my true spiritual self and my family, so why do I keep doing it?

My decision making, which was never my best trait, became terrible at this point. I had a spate of starting a job and just about making six months before I got pissed off with someone and handed in my notice. It was always people-related, looking back. My behaviour was shocking. I started work as a parts administrator with Sam, my old manager, and I quit the job after two days because I felt nervous about doing a different type of job. The reality was that I should have had stability in my life at this moment and all I was doing by leaving all these jobs was reaffirming that I was not good enough. I was letting other people affect my mindset, when I alone decide when I am happy, sad or angry. All this chopping and changing understandably started to affect my relationship with the lady I loved. I was a complete idiot. This was my old pattern of behaviour; I was letting myself down badly and there was a lot of mental self-harm going on. When I was having a discussion or an argument with someone I would think that the other person could see that I was no good; because that was what I felt about myself, that I was no good, or not good enough. So I would go into flight mode, creating a bad argument so I could say 'I've had enough of this job, I am going self-employed again without any capital. Again.'

Sometimes I could catch myself just as I was about to storm out of work and leave the job. I could talk myself round and say 'Slow down, what is wrong?' and calm myself down. These bad habits were deeply entrenched in me. Just when I would think I was making headway I would self combust and want to do what I wanted to do. The most important thing for me was spotting the warning signs early enough so I could calm down and bring myself into the present where I was more rational.

But off the back of several bad decisions I then thankfully made a better one and I then started work as a workshop manager at a truck dealership in the Forest of Dean. I enjoyed the job and my boss, Elliott, was a lovely guy. It was quite an interesting environment, as it was a family company and the owner would come in from time to time to see what was going on, even though his son now ran the business. There were three generations of the same family there and to say that that there were politics was an understatement.

I stayed with the company for nine months but I had the self-employment bug and had the idea of running a recruitment business for the motor trade, as I had loads of contacts. I was also thinking about starting a digital magazine. Katherine was not impressed when I said I was starting my own business again. With no savings or capital it was doomed to fail.

16 EXTREME BEHAVIOUR

I used to be a sucker for extreme behaviour. It was all or nothing, chasing women, drinking to excess or doing drugs in my early twenties. Just as long as whatever I was doing was able to take me out of my manic mind I was happy; I just never coped well when my mind would be having loads of different thoughts. I thought that I had to act out on most of them, and unfortunately that is what I did. I felt like there was a hole in my soul and I used many different external things to fill it, but it did not work. It started to change once I realised I was the only person who could truly make me complete and happy.

Looking back to as far as I can remember, I never felt part of the group; I always felt like I was on the outside looking in. I realise now that a lot of people feel the same way, but they don't act on their feelings;

they learn to engage with people and move through these situations. But with my poor self-esteem and massive ego when I was younger this was not likely to happen; in my mind I thought I was a God, but I also felt like crap most of the time. It was so tiring playing all these characters. I was busy trying to please people, as I was not comfortable in my skin at this point. What I also remember about my time in active addiction was that my hands would shake violently as the adrenalin went through my veins and my head swam with thoughts of how I could win back the money. Gambling was like a drug to me.

17 WORKING MY RECOVERY

After lapsing on 15 November 2012, I went back to
Gambling Recovery meeting the following Thursday
and sought help. I realised that my main problem was
that all I was doing was abstaining from gambling and
not changing my character by working on my
recovery. My life had come to a crisis, as I actually
thought I was going mad. At one point I thought I
must be mad, as I kept self-sabotaging and making
things go wrong; I was unable to stop myself making
the same mistakes. I realised that one of main
problems was that I would almost always act on the
first thought that came into my mind; I never realised
that this was just a thought and that I didn't have to
respond to it. Normally the first couple of thoughts
are the wrong things to do. I reached out to one of
the guys in the group and asked him to be my

sponsor and I started working on my steps slowly.

My sponsor Mark helped me to look at how I was dealing with things in my life. He showed me that I should be doing the right thing and not the right thing for Steve. By practising doing the right thing it helped me with my self-awareness and helped me connect better with other people. I was no longer this Supreme Being in my mind, I was a human being with all the frailties and strengths. I had done work on the Recovery Steps previously, during my initial seven-and-a-half years of abstinence. I had never previously worked through one step at a time, as I thought that not all the steps were relevant to me.

This stuff made me feel awkward and uncomfortable. But now that I had gone through the pain of relapsing and seeing that my life was not really improving, I wanted to try another way. I did find the process very hard at times, and still do. Working on my recovery fully challenges my beliefs. I have to methodically work my way through the steps. In many ways it is important that it takes time to achieve, as real change does take time to happen.

I started on the first Step, admitting I was powerless over gambling, and wrote out my complete gambling history from as far back as I could remember, including the many crazy and self-absorbed things that I had done in the throes of addiction. I remember now that my Step One inventory was about ten pages long. I found the whole process quite cathartic.

I remember doing this around January 2016, and I went through in detail with Mark what I had written in my recovery. Some of these things I had never shared with another person; I did feel very emotional as I was reading out all the things that I had done to myself and to people that I loved. I never felt at any point that I was being judged as I went through all of my pages of content again. Some of the things I was sharing could have been very embarrassing in a different scenario, but I trusted Mark as my sponsor and held nothing back as I moved forwards.

When I had finished talking through the Steps with Mark I had a great sense of unburdening myself, as I had been carrying all this negativity like a great big rucksack on my back. I was now in a position to let go of all these things that I had done, as I was no longer that person; I was evolving into somebody different, somebody more rational, somebody calmer and certainly more connected. I could feel myself wanting to listen more in Recovery meetings and not needing to be right or to ram my opinion down the throats of others as I had done in the past. Other people in the group commented too on how much calmer I appeared to be and that I seemed at peace with myself; I was starting to be on a spiritual journey now.

18 A NEW START IN A NEW CITY

We decided that we would move to Bristol, as my girlfriend, Katherine, wanted a faster pace of life: Cheltenham was not for her. I found work at a car dealership in Bristol and for the first couple of months I was commuting from Cheltenham. That was quite hard going as I was working ten-hour days without the travel.

We moved into the new house just after Christmas 2014. Katherine didn't like the new house, which was my fault as I had chosen it on my own; I thought I was doing the right thing. That was another example of my poor decision-making, which could pop up from time to time. For instance, in the previous five years I had walked out on at least five jobs. The reason for these exits was pure 'fight or flight'; I had poor communication skills with other people and thought that someone was having a go at me. In time, though, I came to realise that these people were only stating their opinion, whereas I had thought they were saying I was wrong or stupid. My mind made everything about me. Thankfully I have learnt from these mistakes. My poor decision-making is much rarer now.

We enjoyed going out in Bristol, as there was a lot more to see and do with ourselves, and I could see us building a new life for ourselves there. It had taken a fair amount of convincing myself that moving to Bristol would be OK, as I am a committed dad to my daughter and didn't want to be too far away from her.

My job was quite stressful, as the Bristol garage was in a mess. The workshop staff were demotivated, customer service was poor and we were flooded with phone calls for parts. I was enjoying the job until our new regional manager, Craig, started. It felt to me as if he had it in for me from day one, but that was only my opinion, and I can see now that Craig had a difficult job to do. Craig had a really bad habit of having a go at me in front of other members of staff, which I really disliked. I found this really demotivating and mentioned to him that I found this behaviour to be unfair and suggested he should take me to one side and talk to me one-to-one if there was a problem. Craig had also brought in a new sales manager, called Tony, and I felt that there was a bullying culture taking shape as they hounded one member of staff was out of the door.

I did not get on very well with Tony, as we would often clash, and sometimes I would fall out with David, one of the salesmen, who could get as excited as me. Craig had remarked that I was the common denominator in all of these issues. Looking back, he may have had a point as I found the environment very aggressive and not one that I wanted to be in. Unfortunately, after an initial busy period things had got quieter in my department, so Craig was on my case big time and, in my eyes, unfairly so. Meanwhile what I saw as staff bullying was getting worse. I had decided that I would do something about it and contacted Craig's boss to speak to him about what was going on. Craig, Tony, the director and I met up the next day to talk about my accusations. Looking back now I wished I hadn't complained, as all that happened was that Craig and Tony said there was no problem. They said I was being too sensitive and that Tony had a job to do.

After that meeting with Craig and the director our relationship broke down completely. I felt as if he was pushing me towards the door and wanted to get his own man in. When I was under this sort of pressure, I still had a tendency of reverting to type, which in this instance was to hand in my notice, get paid and start working on the magazine I was planning in Bristol. I can see now that by speaking to the director and going over Craig's head I had created a situation and made myself open to further criticism. Looking back, I think I almost engineered the situation so that I had to leave. This was only in February 2015. So much for progress.

It was at this time that Katherine told me that I would have to move out of our house in Bristol. I was distraught. I had arrogantly thought that we would always be together but understandably she had decided that I was never going to change. It hit me very hard, because Katherine was the lady I wanted to be with. I was very low, and withdrew into myself, suffering with self-pity and guilt for several months as I loved her very much. Our split was a reality check for me as I realised that I had to stop doing things my way. I had to change for my long-term health.

I ended up moving back to Cheltenham to stay at my mum's till I could sort out a part-time job whilst I built up my magazine. This is what it had come to, 40 years old and living back at home; but I said to myself this is what you have done, accept it and move forward one day at a time. Within a couple of months, I had started a driving job in the evenings, which allowed me to work on the magazine in the daytime.

With working my gambling recovery and being more mindful, I was starting to realise how much work I was going to have to do to stop my mind wanting to destroy everything around me. I could certainly feel the improvements from working on my recovery and I could tell that I now had the ability to look at all the options. I left the job after six months, as working on my own business during the day and then driving in the evening was completely tiring me out. I found myself a job as a business development manager at a cleaning company in Quedgeley. It is a nice company to work for. The owner is a good man and the people there are really cool.

19 WHO AM I?

So who is Steve Taylor? I would like to think that I
know myself quite well these days. I am someone
who is family related and my daughter is always at the
forefront of my mind. I like to try and help others
and I enjoy the company of like-minded people. I still
want to leave a legacy and I have some good ideas
around helping other people around positivity and
self-improvement. It has taken me many years to
identify my true spiritual self and not the ego that
caused me unending problems in my relationships
with others and myself.

I am truly blessed that I am gambling-free.
Without the shackles of addiction, I feel that with
hard work and focus I can still achieve the things I
want to do in life and be proud of who I am. This
journey of self-awareness has not been an easy one

and at times I felt as if I was going to some dark places it would be hard to bounce back from. At one point I even considered seeking psychiatric help. But, as they say, sometimes through adversity you become who you always were. I believe that my repeated mistakes, acting out of addiction and leaving jobs, got me to a point of surrender and acceptance.

So why had I chosen gambling addiction? I asked myself this question many times at the start of my recovery. At the beginning I thought it was about just wanting loads of money and believing that this was the easiest way for me to achieve it. As time went by, and I worked my recovery in more detail, I realised that I had fallen into gambling and it could just as easily have been drink or drugs. My underlying belief was that I was not good enough. I would seek addictive behaviours so I could hide away from day to day life and quieten my manic mind as I struggled to cope with the pressures of life, be that relationships, work or bills. I didn't know what else to do. The gambling then became an emotional crutch. Every time I felt worry or trouble, my brain would say 'You know what you like to do when you feel crap, have a bet.' So in no time at all I was addicted. At times I liked the fact that the only thing I had to think about was how was I going to be able to gamble tomorrow.

This pattern of only thinking of gambling kept me functioning for several years. I didn't think about friendships or relationships. I didn't overly think about my career. All I thought about was how I was going to get money to gamble with tomorrow, and that was it. At times it was just as much of a buzz juggling my money so that bills would get paid and that I could keep my secret life under wraps. I am so glad that this mad lifestyle has ended. It was so stressful. I remember being in a constant state of worry as I knew I would have to make up some story if my girlfriend asked if we could go on holiday or buy something for the house. Now I am blessed that I don't have these worries; I just do my best to deal with the joys of life on a daily basis. It isn't always easy, but practising taking action and being responsible has paid dividends for me.

Once I realised that I didn't have to lead that crazy lifestyle I began to appreciate that I didn't want to self-destruct anymore; I wanted to create myself a good life. I could be proud of how far I had come on my journey as an addict. I am truly blessed that I didn't go to prison or end up homeless or in a mental asylum, as that was the direction that my life was going in. Being happy with where you are in life is the ultimate feeling for me. Living more in the present moment is where I want to be. As I type this paragraph I am not anxious, nor am I depressed, I am happy.

This mindset change from extreme thrill-seeker to

someone who is happy with the balance of everyday life, took me many years, with many failures. But I realised that all my mistakes, and the lessons that I had learned by overcoming these obstacles, had got me to this happy place. What I realised was that life is never straightforward, and that I only seemed to learn by screwing up and putting myself backwards. But now, thankfully, I was living my life the right way.

20 BRIGHT FUTURE

How do I explain recovery to someone who does not attend a Gambling Recovery meeting? It is a spiritual journey for me and a real transformation of personality and thinking, as my decision-making was my biggest downfall. The hardest thing with recovery is that it is gradual and it took me a long time for some parts of my thinking and personality to change. As an example, I have really suffered with false pride, which means pretending that I am someone more important than I am, which is linked to self-esteem.

With practice, I have been able to just be my true spiritual self and realise that I am a normal bloke, trying to make better decisions. Over the years I felt I had made progress with certain parts of my personality, only for it to slip again, as I hadn't been practising my new skills. I needed to learn to be vulnerable with people and stay in contact with people, as being alone in my own mind is a dangerous place. Practising these new skills is so important; as with all new skills you have to make them a habit for them to be embedded into your subconscious mind.

It seems that most compulsive gamblers only focus on abstinence, as in not gambling. Don't get me wrong, that is brilliant, but in my experience I could create untold damage to others and myself by just abstaining from gambling. I needed to change my personality traits so I stopped self-destructing and started to give myself some well-deserved love. Love is so important to me as I spent the best part of 15 years hurting myself and telling myself that I was crap, no good and a loser. I now know that I am a good person who made some decisions that did not work out well for me and that if I could make better decisions my life would improve.

My life is improving day by day. I used to be blinkered to nature, but today I can enjoy the beautiful things in life: a rainbow, birds singing and the wind blowing. It is great to be alive. I also have a new sponsor who helps me work through my recovery and who is there when I need advice and guidance.

Looking back today over the last 25 years of my ongoing battle with gambling addiction, I see me planning my life around the Cheltenham Festival, buying shares in a racehorse, gambling thousands on roulette, losing £90,000 with my first business and all the other madness. Sometimes I think I am lucky to be alive as I realise I was probably only another two or three bad decisions away from being in prison, mental asylum, or living on the streets.

Even with all this self-harm, I would not change a single thing, as I am grateful for the opportunity to repair the faults in my personality and the traits that drove me to do crazy things. I really am lucky that I have managed to move away from the daily hell of addiction and into the wonderful opportunities that are available to me as a recovering compulsive gambler. I am excited about the journey ahead, and have the comfort of knowing that without gambling I was able to find my true self and be happy with the person I saw looking back at me in the mirror.

Steven Taylor
Cheltenham, England, 2017

ABOUT THE AUTHOR

Steve Taylor was born in 1975 in Cheltenham, Gloucestershire. He started gambling at 18 and quickly became addicted. He has been attending a gambling self-help group for 12 years. *Compulsive* is his first book.